Lions Like Us

ALSO BY HOLLIE HARDY

How to Take a Bullet: And Other Survival Poems

Lions Like Us

POEMS

Hollie Hardy

RED LIGHT LIT

Published by Red Light Lit Press
557 8th Ave., San Francisco, CA 94118
redlightlit.com

Library of Congress Control Number: 2024933950
ISBN 978-0-9998895-2-7

Cover Art and Design: Anthony Chase
Book Design and Layout: Anthony Chase and Hollie Hardy
Author Photo: Anthony Chase

For Anthony

Contents

Part 4: Eternal Architecture

Elevator Pitch

Take me home

To ripen and mottle
in the dim light of candles
to open small mouths
and lick like flames
at the edges of you

From the window
of your glass elevator
you flicker like a moth
the city pours its artificial stars
across the silent nightscape

I want to say
pack your suitcase
gather your ghosts
let's live in the ocean like salt
let's build a tree house of wind and sand

Still we wear our chains
rusting like fear
counting our seatbelts
counting the rain

I open my mouth to tell you
how hunger binds us together
how the tether of night unties the moon

I open my mouth
but a wren flies out

I wanted to say
take me home.

This Cherry

PART 1

Storm

The nightscape is a skillet of coffee shops
bone-split patterns of jagged light
a swarm of incorrect sky

Nor can the go that green gives be ignored
these flesh vessels, their slippery delights
your willful promiscuity

We are wet hair, soul-drenched
infused with liquor
we are the sound of rain on roof

Here is a uterus I just know you're going to love
unyielding, purpling, the unraveling of the throat

In a storm that doubles as longing
how we shudder and thrust and ache

Gnaw at the angel's bloody hammer
strain against the rope

Until at last we curl in sleep
in this garden of little letdowns
private animals, guardians of tenderness

There Is No Synonym for Palimpsest

Tonight your heart takes
        the long way home
the way artists learn to be islands
every step feels like
            a confession

You remember
grilled cheese and pickles
        lipstick and treacherous
a sidewalk spectacle   with abandon

Your corrupt cartography
        makes a mentor of wind
a carnage of evidence   your hands
were meant for painting

Here is the night
        dressed in glass
            liquid landscape
        your shadow in a doorway
this is the likelihood
        of losing something

We are always alone
            in the dark
even when we are loving
years unravel us
        like laughter

You sort your longing
into boxes, cigarettes and sentiment
time   slow dances in blue

Freedom is a kind of mythology
      a consolation for danger
the story we tell ourselves
          in the morning

Muse

In the morning
the memory of you
warms like a sun at the center of me

Desire is an old muse
I've discovered
where she keeps her lantern

I try on her dress, gossamer wings
your bedsheet a mirror
we walk through

We hold hands in the ergonomic quiet
watching the sun melt
hearts beating a little too fast

Another Manhattan

Something dark and new
growls inside the night circus
where my heart flutters like a spectacle
in its little cage

The lion the whip and the taste of you
lingers like a season
nicotine and leather
those hands

I've been drinking about my feelings again
here in the forest of us
where everything is newly planted

Are we rocks or air?

The tide of you rolls out
light shines through the doorway
like a message from home

Here is a lesson about truth
sculpted of bricks and glass
here is another Manhattan

I'm trying to be taller again
and you are teaching me to wait
this cherry is not a metaphor
for loss

The way blood prefers to be inside the body
but rushes away at every opening
a kind of defeat by escaping

I want to see the stars again
I want to walk with you in the rain

I wake up with my hands
folded over my chest like a coffin

Sometimes you're here
nestled in the small of my back

And sometimes you're gone

Desire

Today you reappear
on my horizon
a misplaced mirage

All hands and eyes and breath
discovery of ears and toes
will come later

You are late to arrive
because suspense
is a kind of longing

The weight of a tongue
guarding its secrets
gliding along a body

I want to wake up
in the moonlight
of your arms

With the smell of snow
singing in the distance
I want to climb inside

The warmth between us
and build a nest

Nascent

Fragile in our infancy
we wait with our hearts out

Breadcrumbs for birds
I gather pieces of myself

From the ocean
behind your teeth

We forage change from the fountain
in the hypothetically ever after

As if we could take back our wishes
unmake our desire

Bone deep
you saturate me

Every emotion
alive

A new kind of animal
just being born

All quiver and purr
sparkle and fur

New eyes opening
like light

Ephemeral

We play house in a crumbling castle
make-believe with loose-fitting breath

We drink the river
from shattered glass

This body in drenched repose
ribboning like bandages

Remember you still have hands
to paddle this boat we built for now

Dry off your loneliness
you're going to need it

Spooning hunger into the blue
estuaries of strangers, a substitute for longing

Always the poems are about longing

Bruised ink on wet paper
a shipwreck unbecoming

We are lamentations of ghosts
pulsing in our tidal afterglow

We look into the eye of departure
seeking lighthouse, seeking storm

Appreciating the art
of monsters

Their armor, their claws, their iridescent wings
for escaping

I touch your sternum
it's a message you don't understand

A door to a heart with no key
salt is the taste of everything now

Here in the exit lane

Deciduous

Your rope is an apple
in a Magritte sky

Potential and her shadow
the way pronouns change their meanings

You keep calling me
by different names

As we evolve
into   and away

Water is the cure
for everything now

Heart   and distance
eroding the idea of us

Growing a secret forest
of little teeth

Deciduous   falling
another allegory for change

Uncoiled from its ball
does the rope lose its power?

Or stretch   to its full potential
unfurling   its talent for restraint?

What can the rope swing teach us
about sitting still   about letting go?

This thirst, these hungry hands
tied   untied

Reaching   across canyons
now visible   now vanishing

Blue   a study of clouds
a swarm of disappointment

Rushing across your forehead
crashing to earth   Icarus

How readily you accept it
this mouthful of fingers

I hold my breath as we climb
out of the water   out of the well

These tools of erasure
were never   what we hoped for

Sometimes goodnight
feels like forever

Sometimes goodnight
feels like   goodbye

Five More Minutes Please

I had a dream that you were gone
silhouettes of sky where your mouth once was

Alone in the you-shaped chasm, aching in the aftermath
I listen to our soundtrack on repeat

Candles burn the night's edges
your soft snore punctuates the smallest hours
like the shuffling of nocturnal animals

I curl around you
dreaming of breakfast

This moment is all we have, all we ever had
before we break into pieces
thirsty as beach glass

We've been practicing departure
since we met

Tonight I want to be present
in the crook of your neck, the small of your back,
the back of your tongue, the breath in your lungs

Slippery little memories, our bodies
fit together in whispers
naming and claiming and letting go the stars

This sadness is a kind of distance
a shift of light
through winter trees

All of the songs remind me of you
and I want to keep dancing
just a little bit longer

Not What We Expected

PART 2

Disenchanted

Your spell is broken
I bury my memories inside the wound
to soak up the last of my desire

You were always leaving
in spite of the lantern
its emerald ocean

This mouth, these fingers
a dream of mirrors
how tightly I held you

Love is a fickle thing
tenuous in the too-bright light
fragile as a dandelion in winter

Scent of snow and rope burn
I pull the thread and we
unravel

I open my hand
and let the wind take you
like ash

Pillow Talk for One

Here in the rubble of midnight's curtain
I stand my ground

I queen myself a ruler of ledges
and digger of tiny holes

I burn puzzle pieces
to solve mysteries faster

I tie you up with city lights
and make you wait

I fold you neatly
as a little lamb

Rinsed of all expectations
I bite the dark

And savor this sorrow

Let Go or Be Dragged

Out of the darkness and into a fire
a future, a future fire

We are fire burning in rain
things we say in our sleep are held against us

Against the morning, the muscle, the way you move
the way we hurt

Each other. I awake into the past again
all my old boyfriends have married my mother

Now no one can be saved
not even at a discount

Yearning and waiting are
two sides of the same ache

We move out of the dark and into the fire
saving our fears for later

If I soften will I lose my edge
will I melt you

I want to sleep but my bed is on fire so I spread
rumors of my own unmaking, disheveled

I diagram my undo list
digital and complicated and hard to read

In the purple forest of dream
even the rain is burning

These are my resolutions.

Two Doors: Indicative & Allusive

~Ekphrasis after Alex Kanevsky

Door #1

Backlit nudes embrace in the forever light
erasing

Disguises heaped in piles
discarded like dirty petals
stripped down to a single moment
when time stops
like a heart

Still, there are flowers in her hair
skin pressed against skin
arms and hips
her breath on his neck
the stillness of waiting

Doorway or mirror
this closet, a private sorrow

The floorboards of us glow red
embers for eternity

In the aftermath of goodbye
there is no such thing
as goodbye

Door #2

The lights are off in the bedroom

Light is a story you can't unsay
as we crouch alone in the dark

There is no one
sleeping here now
no one staining the walls
with laughter
waking the neighbors
with animal noises
no wild horses
no midnight crackers
no you

All the doors lead to mirrors
reflecting the sound of your voice
as lost island   as lacuna
recalling your body as water
as home

I had a fantasy
you would return
step smiling from shadows
all wisp and whisper
to steal my breath from the room
replace the air in my lungs with flowers
invite the joy of drowning

Instead, little flies
celebrate spring in the garden
box-stepping mindlessly
a jasmine moon rises
glows full

Are they happy?

Do their short little lives
feel long inside such tiny bodies?

I pull the ocean into my mouth again
a thirst to swallow me whole

Repetition & Spectacle

I've been writing the same poem for years
like permutations of wind

There's a boy and a girl
a sky, an ocean, a mouth, a question
where should I begin?

I open my body
to show you its architecture
of indecision

You are the blood and the veins
building a galaxy of warm places

I lay out my bones on the front lawn
like a panoply of whispered secrets

This bone is called fear, this bone is for courage
here is the heart bone, the funny bone
the bone of grief and longing

They are never the shapes you were expecting
oval horse, octagonal lion
the forever shapes of river and home

The edges are smooth as morning coffee
sharp as the day you left me

I make a sign
of submission or defiance
Fire Sale, it reads:

Make me an offer
I can't refuse

Grit

The sting, like stubble, the ache of it
builds a fire of longing inside cataleptic dreams
where I roam the urban ashes of a broken city
searching for sleep

Breath stale with booze at the close of a sweat-damp night
I play the role of a dime store Mata Hari
full of secrets
winking and slinking in ruby shoes
the grit below my smile
gravelly as an old Tom Waits song

Alive in dusty boxes, a dim memory in black and white
pressed between the pages of half-filled journals
I am an ill-fitting little cage of identity
a sometimes-smoldering cinder of shame
both saved and abandoned

I take comfort in the familiar
curtains heavy with nicotine
hollow curve of the bottle
the sound of pigeons
scratching and cooing at first light

I have learned that change is a misdemeanor
in the fragile ecosystem of the body
I have learned what I must do
to fall asleep

Unseen

Perhaps you are the spark
which lures the moth to its glowing demise
igniting the divine

Charred whispers travel the breath
jasmine climbs the night air, teasing
your balsamic laughter, a memory of violence

That which is invisible languishes in abstraction
the texture of smoke, your unconscious bias
I resolve to end a poem without

resorting to sleep. I discover
my mistakes like strange treasures
reflected in the actions of others

The ocean's indifference, relentless
roaring in my smallest bones
the secret ingratitude of sunlight

I lay back in the grass
and let the sky slip over me
like a childhood

I remember how you wanted to be smaller
how you tried to fold yourself into a paper bird
tiny wings full of dark

If they wanted to
all the spiders of the world could band together
to eat all the humans of the world

And when they were done
we would be gone
and the spiders would still be hungry

A Field of Bees

Breakfast, birds sing on the line
sun streams through the kitchen window

Like Rapunzel's hair
cascading from the tower
rewriting the prisoner in new landscape

It's color she remembers
ripe as fruit, the pink of sky
a bridge below, swaying in silent song

Heavy, the weight of a body
ships unfolding the sea
she parts the night to find a heart inside

Here is a small love, the size of a dime
she puts it in her pocket for later

There's a right time for everything, she knows
for dancing or holding one's breath
for walking through a field of bees

The texture of love's voice haunts her now
in the soft outlines of shadows

She conserves light
as a way to begin again
to un-break the egg
taste the new morning

Wasps

Here, take this graffiti heart
brittle as a body bruised with light
almost anything can be a food
if it nourishes

Taste the brine of starting over
shun the broken shortcut
let's throw away our shoes
and feel the earth

Take my hand
we'll go the long way
let desire become sunset and salve
a sex-shaped ache

If distance can be mended
let's drink the poison together
savor its inky bloom
like baby birds struggling to unshell

Even breathing is a risk
these lungs full of anticipation
bombinating like a hive, restless
nameless, bursting with flowers

Collect these little bones
like cast-off wishes
souvenirs of us
bejeweled along the shore

Here, take these fantasies
weightless as wasps
salvaging light from water's edge
waiting, breathless, barefoot in the dark

Temptation

Tonight you speak
the language of floods
tiptoe
on deviant breath
grind against
the dark
sweat-slathered
monster
webbed husk
of your former self
your rogue lips
taste the zipper
ravenous ocean
serrated heart
tease the swollen
machinery of desire
your pearl-
handled tongue
whispers along
the landscape of wrist
nestles in the hollow
of the neck
dreams the roar
of crashing waves

your body is an ache
in the shape of a girl

This Is Not a Horse

Audiences know what to expect, and that's all
they are prepared to believe in.

~*Rosencrantz and Guildenstern Are Dead*

You wake up outside your body
a stick person, a chess piece, a date
with the queen

The last thing you remember is unbuttoning a flannel shirt
letting it fall, to puddle around your feet
like a metaphor

A blue-green ocean parts
inside us, a borrowed bed
we make our own

A wasp kingdom in the garden of winter
where syncopated heartbeats melt like Dalí's clocks
like fireflies discovering snow in the lavender dusk

A sad Leonard Cohen song repeats on memory's turntable
and I Ching pennies clink against the glass
predicting a new journey

We eat salty pancakes and solve crossword puzzles
under a rusty Ferris wheel, where the last embers of night
smell of sex and strange promises

When we wake again, it's raining
and there is a small dark horse
standing in the backyard

This is not what we expected.

The Word for Sky

PART 3

The Orchid Survives

After the glass table
explodes us
back together

We are fragile
as sunlight
on an insect's wing

The glued vase
so easily re-
broken

We speak more
softly now, renewed
a veil of uncertainty

Plays a song of strings
rain and autumn chill
the smell of smoke

Feels like
a warning, but
might just be

Collateral damage
a generational pain
we carry with us

Like the earth
a palimpsest of scars
roots that hold the years

The weight of a thousand
bruised leaves and all the broken
hearts that came before

Restless

So much of love
happens while we wait

On a train
in a forest of arms

Long Distance

Time stretches out between visits
like a dusty road in midsummer

And I am a Cormac McCarthy character
walking away from a broke-down car

With nothing but wildflowers
and empty horizons for company

He loves me. He loves me not.

Because honeybees and rocket ships
are creatures of motion

We count down the days

      T minus 21

           T minus 10

                T minus 7

                    T minus 2

Days ebb in tick-tock rhythms of waiting

What we don't repair, we repeat

So we try to repair our childhoods
while we wait

      just a little bit of poison
      just another breath of water
      just a little longer
      just a little more

I hold on to the hours
of your voice on the phone
find comfort in its tenor of oak and olive green

I pace my apartment
with the lazy diligence of a fly
carving its square dance on the air

      living room, writing room, kitchen

          bedroom, kitchen, writing room, living room

      Hello.
      It's me again.
      I'm still waiting.

We move past small talk to all talk
every moment mourns its slowness

Trapped in a desert
of infinitely recurring symbolism

At the airport, time takes its place
at the back of the line

      I think of the distant future
      I think of the next day
      I think of 5 more minutes please
      I think of how good it will feel

Until finally,

      the seatbelt sign turns off with a bing

         and we all stand up

            like restless babies

               crowding the aisle

Hurry up I think
Hurry up you text

I emerge from the plane
how bright petals burst from succulents
to sudden the air with surprise color

There's still the long walk from the gate

the moving sidewalk, the escalator,

the pit stop, the baggage claim

And then,
at last

you are in my arms
crushing my mouth
with your mouth
hands tangled in hair
tall and short
bent or reaching
finally   embracing

And time

resets itself

Small Moments (A Visit)

Driving sunny back roads
smell of the coast
my fingers in your hair
your too-cold hands warming
between my thighs
Ane Brun's sexy sad songs
predicting another goodbye

Everything is feast
or famine with us
surfeit or dearth
ocean or desert
hunger and thirst

I slip a mint
into your mouth
and you take it
slowly
let my fingers
find your teeth

Even this small act
excites me

Love Poem

A moment of excess
the way clouds taunt rainless

You sacrifice your legs for love
here in the mouth of drought

Where the tongue listens for silence
and drowns in magnificent light

You resolve to forget the sun
electric illusion of safety

Beads of sweat soft-shoe down your spine
like tiny animals seeking shade

You move like a dancer
fingering everything

Every zipper, every fold
every inch of skin

All of the poems are about you
every poem is a love poem

Lighthouse

We draw the shape of loss
on our bathroom mirrors
in dry erase

I traded your body
for the sound of your voice
like water, like coffee

Bitter honey and oak
evening breeze susurrating tall grass
the cat's purr a distant dream

Whispering come closer
whispering come
back

We build a lighthouse of our time together
to contain the wet of sadness
to fuel the fire of hope

Any day now
we will move in
to change the world

You will be the lighthouse
keeper, and I will be
every boat

Saved by your light
or maybe, I'm the rocky
shore, where boats crash

In the sea-
tossed darkness
and you will

Walk along
my banks
like a new moon

Falling

So much happened
    in our imaginations
        skylines and bridges in silhouette
            loneliness wrapped in fog

In what dewy light can we learn to breathe?

            We play a game of hide and seek
      inside a fear of fire

I've been waiting here all along
    ripening like an old polaroid
a camera obscura crouched behind a deepening sky

           I offer you the shadow off my back
      exposed in your net of shade

    We entertain the possibility
        of eternal architecture
           a false promise we sip
               and savor before the storm

        I want to keep you in my gray-green sea
ignore the come-hither motions of mountains and seasons

At night we wallow in sad songs and gastric arias
    weigh compromise and sacrifice
        like love and reckless

        We have nothing
      without the vehicle of the body
    its dark labyrinth
the textures of iron and silk

If I fall over the edge

       of the world

Would you catch me?
    Would you keep me?
        Would you punch holes in the jar

  so I could breathe?

The Dance

We have never had a love
that lasted forever

Yet our wings grow newly each night
soft feathers of hope

You peer into the hollow
wooden belly of a mandolin

There is no music
without emptiness

This muse in small motion
peeling her clementine, eyelashes full of snow

Emblems of dailiness accumulate
life's little meanings

The way clothes hold scent
and scent holds memory

Morning pages, morning run, the soundtrack of us
your wool blanket on the back of the couch

Here is the rift between who we are
and who we'd like to be

Herein lies the importance
of dancing alone

You cling to your rock of agency
uncertainty's moldering refrain

Dried by ocean
drenched in wind

We dance alone
together

As time twirls us closer
quick on its toes

Then flings us apart again

Sleeping Apart at the Seams

In the mouth of our bed
of leaves, you kneel

Pressed fetal
toward sleep

I reach into the void
between us

Where god is not
smoke

Hurts your eyes
and I can almost see

The lions
in your dreams

I reach for the small
of your fear

We're still feeling
our way

Across the vast
dreamscape

Where our bed
is a symbol of solitude

Where our bed is the soft
hammer of love

Super Sad Anniversary Poem

I want to write poems of celebration and sorrow
          because all these poems about longing
                    are probably boring your cat

                         And so the city unpeels itself
                    throws its slick wrapper into the ocean
               careless of heights
indifferent to danger

We only hike uphill these days
          a tough-love reeducation
                    for the breath

                         I learn that in Malay
                    people rise up to love
               instead of falling in
like Americans

And so we give pet names to waterfalls
          like crash and crush, like brio
                    because roar is too cliché
                         for lions like us

                         I miss you in the mountains
                    where the sun licks the sky
               and at night under panoply of stars
alone in my little tent

At home, I miss you in the kitchen, under my dress
          in my empty mailbox, and in the audience
                    especially today

La Lengua de Cielo

I search for home
in the hollows of your body

Where salt blooms like an orchid
and ages like a stone
ancient and solid

We gather our names like seasons
like secrets, like long-term

We learn to be brave
to risk and reveal our most fragile parts

Butterfly wings and wishbones
castles of breath, a sky full of stars
a mouthful of distance

In Spanish the word for language
is the same as the word for tongue

We learn to communicate in waves
water whispering along a body of truth
como salado y mojado, como claro, como luz

My night jasmine sleeps in the daytime
with closed little fists of blooms

Ready to burst into fragrance
at the slightest touch of dusk

I want to find my way home to you
without losing myself in the journey

In Spanish the word for sky
is the same as the word for heaven
is the same as the word for sweetheart

Mi cielo, mi amor
acércate a mi

Types of Blue

Sometimes I miss the pretend
versions of each other we made
up when we met

I think of blue

Light bends the sky
a darker shade of lonely

I think of mountains, fog-colored
spangled with twilight

I admit it, I long to disperse
like ink in water
staining everything wet

I want to stop missing you

Like Maggie Nelson's *sleeve of ash*
falling off a lit cigarette

We are memories of smoke

I decide to start leaving you notes
I write: Darling,
I'm thinking of blue

I want to write a poem that makes you cry
like a Joni Mitchell song
rips the tears right out of your heart
or throat or wherever tears are made

At the blue ballet
the dance about belonging
is actually a story of grief

sad ballerinas consoled in blue light
night air humid with strangers

I think of wolf fur
the true color of winter
Picasso's blue guitar
Joni's melancholy voice

Breaking up
the line
with fresh blue sorrow

You don't notice the imaginary
love notes
I've been leaving you—

I just want you
I write

I just want you to be okay

Blessings Incognito

The specific gravity of your city
crumbles in the rearview, aging in its sleep

As the universe rescinds its privileges
boon by boon

Bricks up your view, like Poe's beating heart
whispering curses in the darkness

Your friends frolic in the debris
of your discarded life

Puddle stomping after the first rain
moving into your apartment

They try on your teeth, your fur
wrap your skin around their shoulders

And you let them—
you make new a list

Of ways to wear white
and how to write a new life

Because even longing can be a kind of happiness
if the ache of it fills you

Like a sail full of wind
galloping toward a hole in the sky

Holding your breath in the tunnel—
you make a new wish

Phoenixing

~For Jessica

I wake up from a dream about a boat
and toss pennies for meaning

You can't be a hero or a mystic by staying home
you must travel and have adventures

The oracle forgets the pandemic
requires a new kind of domestic hero

I think of Icarus again
singed feathers and dirty hands

If I were a boat, I could sail unmanned
nourished by sea-blue and sun alone

In the dream my heart is a door left open
and the boat is a symbol for something unknown

I put my arms around the idea of us
nesting somewhere warm and new

You transmogrify into a migratory bird
bright eyes fixed on a new future

And I am fixing to phoenix again
a woman turning in

To herself

Eternal Architecture

PART 4

Staying Home

I dreamt I was packing a bag
with the names of all the things
and all the people I had lost
the names were scrawled on scraps
of paper scattered across the floor
and the bag was already
too heavy to carry

Awake in the hammer of storm
we cannot experience wetness
only hot and cold
only pressure
I motion you closer

In our collective apocalypse
we can't help reaching for comfort
we can't stop touching
our faces

Streets are quarantine-empty
a new kind of winter or maybe
they're just lonely

I read a study that says sometimes
people think they are lonely
when really they're just cold
so we devise a blanket drive
for the broken-
hearted

While I wait, my eyes are getting old
and so are my hands, my hair, my skin

Maybe my American dream doesn't
have a house or kids, maybe this bridge
is enough   maybe this bridge

                    And you?

Black birds burst across
a silver skyline
like musical notes
golden melody of melted sunlight
city silent in silhouette

Skyscrapers still break the horizon
soft haze mutes the low-slung sun like a lampshade

I keep trying to capture this bridge
like a butterfly
migration
like gratitude

What we prioritize is what we manifest
I scrawl your name on a scrap of paper
I keep trying to keep you   closer

I pack a bag
motion of wings and wishing
I keep trying to define
what home means

(place or person)

With animal bones and ash
carapace or carcass
apotheosis of city
city heartbeat
city girl

Sine Qua Non

Because *every animal longs to be bare*
I'm clearing a space for something new

I discard furniture and habits like unzipped skin
then note my surprise when humans still iron,
smoke, or eat fast food

It's not meant to be judgmental
I just remake the world in my own image
I am perpetually mistaken
about the world

I lie on a borrowed yoga mat, listening to my breath
sine qua non, without which not

My students share with me their fears
of tiny holes and pool drains
their talent for untangling necklaces
they love the smell of rain and gasoline
the buoyancy of balloons enthralls or repels them

Now notice the stillness of the body
how the practice of breathing has opened
a space inside you

Who eats the burlap skin of kiwis
discards the sandpaper soft of peaches
do you prefer the pleasures of skin or flesh?

We assemble our idiosyncrasies
to make of them a kind of joy

In yoga there are eight limbs
pranayama controls the breath
pratyahara withdraws the senses

As darkness brightens the light
and even lentils fetch delight after a fast

The way weeks of abstinence electrify
your longing, your lips, your breath

The way fern fronds shiver
when you blow on them

Fallout

At first, your exit plan did not include me
now we're taking it day by day

Sheltering in place means sleeping
late, slow coffee mornings

Alive with chattering birds
empty planes drone overhead
divinity in a deepening sky

Let's not talk about this
bread and this wine
building my new home-body

Routine forms around opening curtains
wiping down light switches
we ration toilet paper, reorganize the fridge

We hike mountains in defiance
bask in the bounty of urban foraging
tiny trespasses in strangers' gardens

Used masks hang like fruit bats in the west window
houseplants shift toward light
like us, the sun tracks our happiness

So many poems about impossible love
and now you're here, in my apartment

Neither of us knows what will happen next
we never do

Slow Motion Upon a Pallid Landscape

Days slide nameless into weeks
Tuesday tantamount to Saturday

Is it the window or the view that matters?

We wake up in fragments hours later than we meant
the sound of hammering is loud at the epicenter of change

We linger in dreams, follow kinks in the hose
pick fruits and flowers that don't belong to us

Happiness resembles a fickle flitting bird

Because quarantine is equivalent to quagmire
we invent a new vocabulary for togetherness
a private lexicon for latchkey adults
a grist of sodium chloride

We eat chocolate at midnight because feelings
are so emotional

We learn to breathe in protest
through our homemade voluntary bindings
but forget to hydrate

We let wind quench our thirst, cooling and tangling
everywhere light lands lush with texture
along the forbidden trail

Waves burst around rocks like wings
poison oak blooms at our elbows
a landslide of hornets

We defy the signs, summit the makeshift mountain because we will not be warned.

We have come to build.

A Murmuration of Starlings

In the cities, protestors break quarantine and windows
expressing moral outrage like a choreographed ballet
at 44, your mother asks you to move home
so she can keep you safe

I take all day to summon the courage
to swim across the river
where the late afternoon
sun warms the rocks

A mother's job is to worry
because we cannot
escape the river, we cannot escape
the president

Hark, the darkening view
from my apartment, television-blue skyline
rearranging a racial hierarchy
hospitals dressed in death

Water is stronger than rocks
time's carving knife ripples
and recedes in its own image
patient, a river-shaped handprint

At midnight, the landlord is summoned
to eradicate a pyre of cardboard boxes
to prevent its burning by protestors (like us)
we enjoy the sight of his labors from behind closed shades

Today, a rocket launches two astronauts into space
escaping gravity but not quarantine
on the ground a handsome reporter
tears up and turns away

In another life, I wonder what kind of bird I might be
built for speed or endurance, solitary or gregarious
I want to join a migration, a murmuration
of starlings, an acrobatic aerial display

On the drive to the river, we play "I'm going on a trip"
you bring an anvil and a parachute
because the laws of attraction
supersede the laws of physics

In the morning, the scent of you
coffee and earth, the promise of rain
the weight of your body next to mine
means you are still here, means I am not alone

Revising America

This heart is a rat-
king knotted with tales
of injustice

Blood-brown as a river
we wade in
like a weapon
like a rocket-
shaped life raft

Ready to revise, to lie
to lie still

Or fight back with fists
with words
with laws
without

This heart is a mural
painted over wood
painted over broken glass
fists raised in unity

This mural depicts your mother
holding the hand of another
she folds herself into a paper plane
she flies herself into
the crowd

We are alone in mountain starlight
at night the wind growls
through the tent, pretends
to be a bear, we hold our breath

This thin fabric pretends
to protect us
promises and lies
we revise our objectives

To be more inclusive
from a distance

Outside our country, unmarked
police begin to disappear
dissenters. By outside
I mean inside. I mean

Here in America

And what power
do we have to stop it?
we ask ourselves
we ask the walls

As we shelter
in place
viewing the world
through Zoom windows
we zoom into our cells

Our cell phones, our oculi
all witness and bristle
we cower on our couches
wondering what will happen
we think we must
take action

This heart is a baby raven
we save, but it only lives a week
just long enough to love
its inky iridescence

We don't let these
little losses ruin us

This heart is a protest
standing its ground
bodies in the streets
she puts on her mask

She folds herself into the fabric
a fist, a promise, a heart
a heart-shaped
knot

Sprezzatura

The breath bent / backward under / foot / a foot trail / entrails
trailing / like lost keys / like next time / like normal is something
we can agree on / missing

Our own personal / normal / ruptured like / overripe plums
the sidewalk a vulture / in wait / in this city / a sidewalk is a bed
without a home

We walked past bodies / in rumpled repose / looking for lost items
finding lost courage / we looked away / we did not do / enough

(Re)Imagine(Nation)

I look up
changed, unbroken
by silence

You become
my self-portrait
in red

A child climbs over
the fence and into
the war

She says go ahead and start
listening
I'll bill you later

The way love
in isolation
is self-love

A stone in each hand
is not the same
as a bird in flight

Why do we insist
on killing birds
in every idiom?

You are the riot
under the flood
crashing

Through my dreams
like a tidal wave
pool-blue and permanent

Our own private ending
in my dream the bird
escapes the cage

Too late
only the spider
survives

Its pale heart beating
like the memory
of wings

A child is born
into smoke
an aftermath

We reimagined, but
politics still won the war
against the earth

And we all lost
and we all lost
and we are all

The child
and we are all
the children

Killing birds

Who We Are Now

The smallest suggestion of skirt
bare legs and secrets
on the bottoms of her feet

Written by an imprecise hand
smeared, archival by daylight

We argue about color
about sepia tones
and flesh tones

About severed hands
in the garden

Every crevice
and fold of skin
reveals her age

A warrior on horseback, that blur
between now and young

The goldfish are more alive
than the rest of us
oranging the bathtub water

The smooth surface of old porcelain
elides their memory of earth

Reshaping their world
the way humans
are always changing

Undressing and reinventing
the skyline

Where Shall We Begin

I'm thinking about change again / as the world bares / its teeth
and snarls / we cower and grumble / or march with balled fists
into the throat of the next war / already begun / as we look
the other way / watching lies on the news / hoarding toilet paper
for the end days

I'm thinking about changing again / as my defaults shift tectonic
my nightlife goes to bed early now / cold neon unblinks
its distant pink / this urban existence on hold / all jackhammer
and no green

We live inside a fishbowl now / so I become my own chef / a new
kind of gourmet / crafting every ingredient / from ether and earth
heat and salt / a small savory body / words for genuflection

A helicopter interrupts again / rumble struts its circle / aims
its giant all-seeing eye / facial recognition / and police
are standing by

I'm thinking about trading my city / for terra incognita / a new
life with a view / we cast our hopes for rain / upon an altar
of tenderness / practice suspense on Saturdays / hold the posture
of dreaming / rooted in windows and hipbones / the many rivers
and levers of the body

I want to see myself newly again / a mirror reflecting music
Ocean says good poetry / is about asking the right questions
what I want to know is—

Where shall we begin?

The Voyeurs

Your life
arches its back, glows golden
in unwashed light
        shifting like stained glass

Goodbye
        is the word that clenches
the keys of change, the sound of metal
        turns
in the door of the poem

The poem turns
        on its axis
like an aftermath

A train purrs across a snowy mountainside
        exhaling soft breath
in the distance a red barn
whispers about war

I want to be the slick black feather
        of a swan molting
against its will, grasping
at refracted light

The poem turns
on itself
inside the cathedral
        someone slices
soap for your anonymous pleasure

You turn on
        mortifications
even evolution is being
        televised

you revise your life
      with lavender

The hay holds an earthy animal aroma
lurid and damp, you can't sleep
      so you watch
foxes frolic in haptic softness

In the dream
you've been standing here
      all of my life
wrapped in curtains
of moonlight

You turn off the news
I turn on the poem
now everyone is staying home
      to watch

The Body

Don't listen when strangers ask you
who the hell you think you are

You know who you are
Icarus

Wherever you go
you hear the flapping of wings

Your body stranded
in sky

All night I dreamt the crow
who fell from flight

Sudden suicidal descent
crashing and crunching

Broken body still warm
my fingers soothing

You are not alone, I whisper
faint throb of life receding

We cry over you
under a waxing gibbous moon

The sheen of your still eye
slays me, an iridescent ruin

Unfurling my faults
a body drowning in air

One for sorrow
we sing farewell

Memento mori for
everyday mortality

At dawn we bury you
beneath redwood roots

We know who we are
we too are made of wax

Spiders Bandaging Prey

Willow breath and broken tines
color the rippling stillness

We haven't washed the windows
since 1997, maybe not even then

We organize our days like paper dolls
treading the watery path
home and away

Stepping on or over sidewalk cracks
according to our disposition for meanness

Our desires are invisible animals
taunted by wind

The city offers comfort
in numbers and distraction
but leaves a residue of guilt

A schedule of unlikely resolutions
slippery mouths and mornings after

I like to imagine my former lives
like layers of tissue paper
wrapped around a forgotten gift

You are there too
writing a love poem by the river
making moonshine in the bathtub
handing out smallpox blankets to the neighbors

Why do we insist our past lives were heroic
or famous?

At four I discovered my hands again
alien and familiar
like the tether of dreams
the wings of birds

My Tongue Is a Trojan Horse

I dreamed I cut open an avocado and inside
was another avocado with bright yellow skin

I climbed the tree of my childhood and fell through
the branches, the fruit of a lie

I never learned what it means to be Chippewa
I looked to the past for meaning

But found only monsters and ghosts
dirt floors and outhouses, moonshine and violins

I tried to tell you about the avocado
but you didn't understand

You learned that scarcity breeds violence
but the death of each chicken haunted you

Like the story of my great-great-uncles who swapped families
each preferred the other's wife and four children

So they traded, there is no moral here
we must make our own meaning

In the photo album, grandma's secret lovers are all torn
from view, one arm resting on the shoulder of a lie

I've cultivated my urban roots, climbing down into the dark
heart of the city, where poetry remembers its origins

Labyrinthine and messy, you open me
juice runs from my heart like a plum

In the dream, someone said you should move back here
and I said, I've never lived here

I cut open the second skin, but it was empty inside
there was no avocado

A Murder of Crow's Feet

~In support of Reproductive Rights and Texas Mutual Aid

I turn down the volume of my internal monologue
so I can't hear the stop signs

Green light in the trees moves like water full of wind
the nap refuses to take, and I toss in uneasy daylight

Sometimes I'm jealous of my old life, my younger body
the enthusiasm of smooth skin, how quickly I healed then

No one got shot
but everybody got hurt

How easily we dismiss our non-material injuries
because emotional trauma cannot be quantified

Dreams, triggers
how we startle at shadows now

You got your stuff back, so you're ok, be grateful
this gratitude moves like water, slips between fingers

The glass both full and empty
like Schrödinger's imaginary cat

If art is an exercise in critical feeling
an act of homolinguistic translation

I stretch out into my new life
barefoot, but not pregnant

I give thanks to my scars and put on my boots
the day smells warm, like sunlight on skin

It is mine to decide
I am the author

The autobiography
of my choices

How to Bask in Anything

Dragonfly shadows bask
on end-of-summer grass

Every-colored bodies bask on blankets
women with their breasts out

Pink toenails and unshaved legs
last night's mosquito bites

I bask in midday bird chatter
lazy river glitter-beckons below

I'm nervous to swim alone. Not of drowning
but a strange embarrassment, like a fear of dancing
not fear exactly, a kind of shyness

The girls with their tops off remind me of my first time
topless on the beach at Cannes La Bocca
the leering Nigerian men selling wooden horses

The way women learn to look away from discomfort
ignore catcalls and unwanted touch

I used to sunbathe naked on the roof of my apartment
not caring if anyone saw me, until I embarrassed a neighbor
and learned that half the sex offenders in Oakland
lived across the street

Now in middle age with my top on
I read poetry and build my courage
there are parts of me that don't need sun

Privilege is feeling brave for entering water
without a comfort animal

I misread youth
as the small town of my mouth

Stretch out into the uncomfortable
identify my resistance, bask in it

I don't think resistance is baskable, said the student
in the act of resisting

The water is cool
and I am feeling brave

In poetry, I counter
one can bask in anything

Awkwardness, a breadbasket full of plastic babies, the liquid
eyeball of god's smallest creature, summer's dirty feet,
the taste of rust on the robber's chain, the one he used to lock up
your stolen bike, a teenage memory of strawberry hairspray, its
sticky aroma a harbinger of swollen nights.

I bask in the ice cube at the edge of your bourbon dream
another wet escape

Already melted, already sucked dry

Here's to You

Because you are amphibious by day and amorphous by night

Because you are running to catch the train

Because you are polished by the furs of countless bears

And riddled with tiny holes

Because you are the murmur and coo of doves

And the smell of pages turning

Your fragrance is monsoon petrichor

Your fragrance is winter campfire

Because you are new-car-scented

And jaywalking in front of police

Because you are a soft place for squirrels to nest

Because you are the click and whir of a zip tie locking into place

Because you stole the pen

Because you are performing your ritual dance

You are humming an illegible tune

You are wet eyes and the crunch of dry leaves

Because you are frosted like a mini-wheat

You taste like moonlight and distance

Your flavor is lemon zest

You are a lion in silhouette

Rising up from the sea

Because you are light years away

From the window

You are petals floating in wind

You are wading in the wishing pool

You are prehistoric and prehensile

You are sipping dandelion wine

Because you are a copy of yourself

Multiplying exponentially

Because you refuse to relinquish the hot tub

And you can no longer resist the pizza

Because you are sharp-toothed and ravenous

Because you are imperfectly perfect

Because you are mine

Here's to you.

Notes

"Repetition & Spectacle" appropriates the phrase "a galaxy of warm places" attributed to *The New York Times* op-ed columnist David Brooks, who uses it to describe comfort zones of political discourse.

"Grit" adapts an "ill-fitting little cage of identity" from the essay "Insatiable" by Mark Doty.

"Types of Blue" references the phrase, "a sleeve of ash falling off a lit cigarette" from Maggie Nelson's book *Bluets*.

In "Phoenixing," the line "You can't be a hero or a mystic by staying home / you must travel and have adventures" paraphrases a modern translation of an I Ching oracle from *ichingonline.net*.

"Sine Qua Non" borrows the phrase "every animal longs to be bare" from Kaveh Akbar's poem "Long Pig" in his book *Calling a Wolf a Wolf*.

"A Murder of Crow's Feet" was written for Boots on the Ground, a reading to protest Texas' 2021 abortion ban and raise funds for abortion mutual aid for several Texas-based organizations fighting for reproductive justice, including Buckle Bunnies, Fund Texas Choice, and Jane's Due Process. The lines "No one got shot / but everybody got hurt" paraphrase a moment from "Motherless Child," season 1, episode 10 of *Clarice*.

"Here's to You" appropriates the phrase "polished by the furs of countless bears" from a greeting card collage designed by visual artist Chris Kenny, and "you can no longer resist the pizza" is from early 2000's infamous anonymous internet troll "bloodninja."

Acknowledgments

Thank you to the editors of the publications where versions of these poems first appeared, sometimes under different titles:

Bay Area Generations: "La Lengua de Cielo," "Spiders Bandaging Prey," "Unseen"

Colossus Press: "A Murder of Crow's Feet," "(Re)Imagine(Nation)"

Dispatches from Quarantine: "A Murmuration of Starlings," "Slow Motion Upon a Pallid Landscape"

Fourteen Hills: "Grit"

Grace Cathedral: 2023: The Year of Poetry Anthology: "A Field of Bees"

Migozine: "Staying Home"

Moonstone Center for the Arts 24th Annual Poetry Ink Anthology: "Sprezzatura"

Passionfruit Review: "Five More Minutes Please," "Long Distance"

Red Light Lit Press: Love Is the Drug & Other Dark Poems: A Poetry Anthology: "Another Manhattan (Finite Is Not a Metaphor for Fire)," "Elevator Pitch"

Samizdat Literary Journal: "Storm"

Deep, heartfelt gratitude to my first readers, Tracy Artson, Jessica Hardy, Heidi Kasa, Jennifer Lewis, Tomas Moniz, Elisa Salasin, and Tess Taylor, who provided thoughtful and essential manuscript feedback; to Tongo Eisen-Martin, Jeannine Hall Gailey, Deborah Landau, Tomas Moniz, Brynn Saito, Maw Shein Win, Kim Shuck, Tess Taylor, and Matthew Zapruder for reading (and writing about) advance copies of the book; to my generous and supportive publisher, Jennifer Lewis, for believing in my work and giving this book a home with Red Light Lit Press; to Sam Caine, Kathryn Rogers, and Jessamyn Violet for their editorial notes; to Cassandra Dallett, Heidi Kasa, Loria Mendoza, and K.R. Morrison for their friendship and encouragement; to my wonderful students and literary community; to my former teachers at San Francisco State University; to the writers and listeners of Saturday Night Special: A Virtual Open Mic for being an inspiration, an audience, and a sanctuary during the pandemic and beyond; to Erin Hudson, Donald Morey, and Susan Morey for being my champions and first listeners for every poem.

To Anthony Chase for moving my desk in front of the window, reminding me to put what matters most first, for the beautiful original cover artwork and book design, for believing in my poetry, for being the love in every love poem. This book doesn't exist without you.

In loving memory of Fred Clinton, who was always my biggest fan. I miss you, Fred.

Reader, thank you.

About the Author

Hollie Hardy is a writer, educator, and author of *How to Take a Bullet: And Other Survival Poems* (Punk Hostage Press) winner of the 2016 Annual Poetry Center Book Award at San Francisco State University. She holds a BA in Creative Writing and an MFA in Poetry from San Francisco State University, teaches private writing workshops online, and hosts the long-running monthly reading series Saturday Night Special: A Virtual Open Mic. Her work has been nominated for a Pushcart Prize and published in numerous anthologies and literary journals including *Bay Area Generations, Colossus, The Common, Dispatches from Quarantine, Eleven Eleven, Fourteen Hills, Migozine, Milvia Street Journal, Parthenon West Review, Passionfruit Review, sPARKLE & bLINK, Transfer,* and elsewhere. She lives in Austin, TX. Learn more at: holliehardy.com

Praise for Lions Like Us

"In *Lions Like Us*, as the poet herself writes, 'every poem is a love poem'—to others, and to the world itself. Reading this book is like falling in love, then parting, then returning to the beloved, again and again and again. Reader, enter to weep, to laugh, to find solidarity. Enter to find, in its purest, most intense, most direct and available form, poetry."

~Matthew Zapruder, author of *Story of a Poem*

"With sparkling, spell-like language, *Lions Like Us* guides us through love-haunted spaces where desire is alive in the wake of sorrow and loss. These poems are tidal and tender; they feel into tectonic cultural shifts while remaining close to the 'emblems of dailiness' that make life meaningful: a mint slipped in a mouth, sweat down the spine, one body leaning into the salt of another. I'm in awe of the quivering architecture of these poems, where nights are 'dressed in glass' and the 'soft / hammer of love' pulses through the dream's roar. Hardy is a poet of surprise and precision with an oceanic heart."

~Brynn Saito, author of *Under a Future Sky*

"There are those stories from childhood about brooding and powerful women who live in difficult to get to places: Hollie Hardy's poetry is what happens to those stories when they grow up and become poems. If I quoted all of my favorite lines and references we'd be here all day. These poems, as Hardy herself, are a bouquet of the unexpected, a defibrillator for whatever organ it is that lets you reel in wonder."

~Kim Shuck, 7th Poet Laureate of San Francisco Emerita

"Hollie Hardy's poetry is an intersection of multiple dimensions of wisdom, both spirit and metallic, personal and populist, song and rattle. In these lines of brilliant observation, you find an impossible absence of the monarchies of time and place usually necessary for assertion. And the ghosts looking over your shoulder will also be sent to the memories of our deepest loves and losses. A manuscript of ether comedown; enjoy the spell."

~Tongo Eisen-Martin, Poet Laureate of San Francisco

"How do we balance love with loss? How do we balance private joy with public pain? In jagged, always unexpected verses, in which 'the nightscape is a skillet of coffee shops' and 'no one can be saved / not even at a discount' we meet Hollie Hardy's old muse, desire, and watch her light her lantern on these thorny, insoluble, but ultimately fascinating questions. Lit by her light, we 'learn to be brave / to risk and reveal our most fragile parts' and 'let [our] heart[s] take the long way home,'—returning the better for it. This is a book to savor."

~Tess Taylor, author of *Leaning Toward Light*

"Hollie Hardy's second full-length collection, *Lions Like Us*, pulses the reader through the pangs of love in mergence and severance, in delicate attempting and ravening tenacity, in 'uncertainty's moldering refrain' and 'ships unfolding the sea' that 'salvag[e] light from the water's edge.' Hardy conveys a tender ferocity that invites the reader to encompass self, other, nature, city, strength, vulnerability, and injustice for what they are, and in so doing to stand, act, and roar from the sovereignty of the heart's courage."

~Maw Shein Win, author of *Storage Unit for the Spirit House*

"Defiant yet vulnerable, sensual yet brutal, the poems in Hollie Hardy's *Lions Like Us* make you feel. The book explores loss and miscommunication; it celebrates promise and possibilities; it looks to community while illuminating the personal and intimate. These poems roar and sing."

~Tomas Moniz, author of *All Friends Are Necessary*

"The exuberant poems in Hollie Hardy's *Lions Like Us* embrace spiders, starlings, and wasps in a cityscape that bustles with lost love and police helicopters alike. She uses the languages of science, philosophy, and advertising to build a universe that holds hope and danger, fantasy and feral ferocity."

~Jeannine Hall Gailey, author of *Flare, Corona*

"Intimate and vulnerable, lyrical and lush, Hollie Hardy's second collection of poems offers gorgeous consolation in our time of crisis. Amidst streets that are 'quarantine-empty,' *Lions Like Us* invents 'a new vocabulary for togetherness,' conjuring love as a haven in a broken world. 'Every poem is a love poem,' she writes, 'The weight of your body next to mine / means you are still here, means I am not alone.'"

~Deborah Landau, author of *Skeletons*